my friendly neighborhood

Farmer

Published in the United States of America by Cherry Lake Publishing
Ann Arbor, Michigan
www.cherrylakepublishing.com

Reading Adviser: Marla Conn MS, Ed., Literacy specialist, Read-Ability, Inc.
Book Design: Jennifer Wahi
Illustrator: Jeff Bane

Photo Credits: © Gena Melendrez / Shutterstock.com, 5; © Pressmaster / Shutterstock.com, 7; © Sursad / Shutterstock.com, 9; © Olexandr Panchenko / Shutterstock.com, 11; © Rawpixel.com / Shutterstock.com, 13; © Gpointstudio / Shutterstock.com, 15; © Syda Productions / Shutterstock.com, 17; © Bbernard / Shutterstock.com, 19; © Smereka / Shutterstock.com, 21; © zhu difeng / Shutterstock.com, 23; Cover, 2, 3, 6,12, 14, 24, Jeff Bane

Library of Congress Cataloging-in-Publication Data

Names: Devera, Czeena, author.
Title: Farmer / by Czeena Devera.
Other titles: My friendly neighborhood.
Description: Ann Arbor : Cherry Lake Publishing, 2018. | Series: My friendly neighborhood | Includes index.
Identifiers: LCCN 2017029643| ISBN 9781534107205 (hardcover) | ISBN 9781534108196 (pbk.) | ISBN 9781534109186 (pdf) | ISBN 9781534120174 (hosted ebook)
Subjects: LCSH: Farmers--Juvenile literature.
Classification: LCC S519 .D48 2018 | DDC 630.92--dc23
LC record available at https://lccn.loc.gov/2017029643

Printed in the United States of America
Corporate Graphics

table of contents

About the author: Czeena Devera grew up in the sweltering heat of Arizona surrounded by books, quite literally as her childhood bedroom had built-in bookshelves constantly overflowing. She now lives in Michigan with an even bigger library of books.

About the illustrator: Jeff Bane and his two business partners own a studio along the American River in Folsom, California, home of the 1849 Gold Rush. When Jeff's not sketching or illustrating for clients, he's either swimming or kayaking in the river to relax.

People eat. They eat vegetables. They eat fruits. Farmers grow these things.

What are your favorite foods?

Some farmers grow **crops**. They grow wheat. Some wheat is turned into bread.

What do you put on your bread?

Some farmers grow **cotton**. Some cotton is turned into **fabric**. This is used to make backpacks and clothes.

Some farmers raise animals. They raise chickens. People eat eggs from chickens.

Farmers sell what they grow. They sell what they raise. Some sell to a grocery store. Some sell at a **farmers' market**.

Where does your family buy food?

Farmers plan. They plan for bad weather. They plan for changing food prices. They plan the next **season**.

Farmers need land. They need land to grow crops. They need land to raise animals.

Farmers use different machines. Some help them **harvest** crops. Some help farmers feed the animals.

Farm work can be unsafe. Farmers must stay **alert**. They must pay attention.

Farmers work hard. They help bring food to everyone's table.

What would you like to ask a farmer?

glossary

alert (uh-LURT) paying attention to what is around you and being ready to act

cotton (KAH-tuhn) a plant that produces seed pods containing fluffy white fibers; also the cloth made from such fibers

crops (KRAHPS) plants grown for food or for sale

fabric (FAB-rik) cloth or material

farmers' market (FAHRM-erz MAHR-kit) a place where people buy food or other goods from farmers

harvest (HAHR-vist) to gather crops from a field

season (SEE-zuhn) a part of the year during which growing conditions for crops are the most ideal

index